THE MINDFUL ENTREPRENEUR

ACHIEVING SUCCESS IN THE WELLNESS INDUSTRY

ABBY FALOY

CONTENTS

INTRODUCTION

A wellness entrepreneur is a businessperson or an individual who produces goods or services that encourage health, fitness, and general well-being. They are enthusiastic about healthy living and assisting others to reach their objectives in terms of their physical, mental, and emotional health.

Wellness entrepreneurs establish their firms in numerous industries, including nutrition, exercise, mental health, meditation, natural cures, and more. Their goods and services include natural supplements, organic foods, yoga courses, psychotherapy, spa services, and wellness vacations, among others.

These businesses concentrate on delivering holistic solutions to enhance their customers' lives by addressing diverse elements of their physical, mental, and emotional well-being. They employ scientific knowledge, competence, and creativity to promote natural remedies that may help prevent or manage illnesses or disorders. Moreover, wellness entrepreneurs play an important role in the present period, when individuals have grown increasingly involved in improving their lives and health. As such, the wellness market is developing fast and drawing more investments, making it a potential business prospect for entrepreneurs.

In essence, wellness entrepreneurs are business-minded

people who utilize their love for health and well-being to promote natural remedies for different health conditions. They play a key role in assisting people to live healthier lifestyles and enhancing the quality of the wellness business.

These are some reasons why wellness entrepreneurship is vital:

I. Supports Healthy Lifestyle: Wellness entrepreneurship encourages the adoption of healthy lifestyles by people. Wellness entrepreneurs produce goods and services that help individuals reach their health objectives. By offering nutritious food, supplements, exercise programs, meditation, and other wellness-related services, wellness entrepreneurs encourage healthy habits in individuals.

2. Improves Public Health: The growth of wellness businesses has led to an increase in public awareness of health concerns. This knowledge correlates to enhanced public health as individuals become more cognizant of the need for regular exercise adequate diet, stress management, and healthy behaviors. With more individuals adopting healthy practices, there is a drop in chronic illnesses such as diabetes, heart disease, obesity, and even mental disorders such as sadness and anxiety.

3. Creates Jobs: Healthy entrepreneurship can generate additional employment in the economy. As the business expands, more individuals are educated to offer wellness services, and more organizations are founded to fulfill the rising need for wellness services. This, in turn,

provides more jobs, promotes economic development, and reduces the rate of unemployment

4. Increase Economic Activities: Health entrepreneurship has become a key driver of economic activity in many nations. Wellness entrepreneurs produce innovative goods and services, which generate money and boost economic activity. By doing so, they contribute to the expansion of the economy and the generation of wealth.

5. Handles Social Problems: Wellness entrepreneurship may help solve some of the important socioeconomic challenges impacting communities globally, such as social inequity, poor health outcomes, and environmental degradation. By offering wellness services to marginalized areas, wellness entrepreneurs may assist to lessen health inequities among the population.

In conclusion, wellness entrepreneurship influences people, communities, and society favorably. The sector works to enhance physical, emotional, and mental well-being, increase economic activity and solve social concerns. Its value continues to rise as more individuals adopt healthier lifestyles.

CHAPTER ONE

DEVELOPING A WINNING MINDSET

The power of positive thinking is a notion that believes optimism may transform our attitude to life, our perspectives, and our mental and physical health. Proponents of positive thinking claim that by concentrating on good ideas, we may bring about positive consequences and enhance the quality of our lives.

These are a few ways in which the power of positive thought may work:

I. Lowering stress and anxiety: Positive thinking may work as a natural stress reliever. By concentrating on happy ideas, we may minimize cortisol, a hormone that generates stress in the body.

2. Improved resilience: A good mindset may help us bounce back from stressful situations. By having a positive perspective, we may discover methods to overcome problems and hurdles and go ahead

3. Improved confidence: When we feel good about ourselves and our talents, we naturally feel more confident. This confidence may lead to greater success in our personal and professional life.

4. Better physical health: Positive thinking may have a favorable influence on our physical health as well. It may help lower blood pressure, boost immunological

function, and improve overall cardiovascular health.

5. Improved connections: A cheerful mindset may lead to better, more meaningful relationships. By concentrating on positivity, we can communicate more effectively and offer and receive love and support more freely.

Harnessing the power of positive thought is vital to cultivate mindfulness and self-reflection. This might entail actively adjusting your mentality to concentrate on happy ideas, adopting a daily gratitude practice, and making an effort to surround yourself with good people. Ultimately, the strength of positive thinking rests in the fact that it helps us take charge of our lives, develop happiness, and unleash our full potential.

Overcoming Self-Doubt and Fear

Overcoming self-doubt and fear in building a winning attitude is important in wellness coaching. Yet, allowing these emotions to govern your thinking might impede you from attaining achievement and creating a winning attitude. To overcome self-doubt and fear, it is necessary to understand how they influence you and create techniques to handle them.

1. Identify the root of your self-doubt and fear
Self-doubt and dread typically arise from prior experiences and may be provoked by specific events or persons. Try to discover the root of your self-doubt or fear and understand how it affects you. This might help you build techniques to control these feelings.

2. Challenge negative thoughts

Negative thoughts lead to self-doubt and dread. To overcome these emotions, challenge negative thoughts by focusing on positive affirmations. Focus on your strengths and accomplishments rather than your weaknesses.

3. Set achievable goals

Setting achievable goals can help you build confidence and overcome self-doubt and fear. Start with minor objectives and build towards more demanding ones. Appreciate your victories along the road, no matter how modest they may be.

4. Employ positive self-talk

Positive self-talk is an excellent technique to overcome self-doubt and fear. Replace negative self-talk with positive affirmations. Employ statements like "l can accomplish this: "l am competent," and "l am confident."

5. Surround yourself with positive people

Surrounding oneself with encouraging individuals may help you overcome self-doubt and fear. Positive friends and family members may motivate you to reach your objectives and give support when you need it.

6. Learn from failure

Failure is a part of life, and it may be a wonderful learning experience. Instead of seeing failure as a bad experience; embrace it as a chance to learn and improve. Evaluate what went wrong, and build a strategy to prevent making the same error in the future.

In conclusion, creating a winning attitude means

overcoming self-doubt and fear. By understanding the root of these feelings, confronting negative beliefs, making reasonable objectives, practicing positive self-talk* surrounding yourself with positive people, and learning from failure, you may create the confidence and resilience required to accomplish success.

Understanding Failure as a Learning Opportunity

Failure is often perceived as a negative outcome, but it is essential to understand it as a learning opportunity. It is a natural part of life and a crucial aspect of personal and professional growth. When we fail, we have the opportunity to reflect* analyze, and learn from our mistakes, which can help us to improve and succeed in the future.

Failure offers an opportunity to understand our limitations and weaknesses, which allows us to identify areas where we need to develop further. As we reflect on our failures, we can gain valuable insights into our behavior, attitudes, and decision-making processes. This introspection helps us to identify the root cause of our failures and understand what we need to do differently in the future.

Aside from self-reflection, failure gives a learning opportunity by requiring us to interact and seek feedback. When we fail, we have to collaborate with others to overcome the setback. This partnership improves communication and teamwork skills, which are necessary for every area of life. Getting criticism from others enables us to obtain a new perspective and find areas where we may improve.

Moreover, failing enables us to build resilience and tenacity, which are vital attributes in life. We learn to accept failures, adjust to changes, and endure despite hardships. This perspective helps us to manage stress and pressure well, which is vital for personal and professional success.

Lastly, failure encourages us to create a growth mentality, which is crucial for ongoing learning and progress. A growth mindset permits us to perceive setbacks as chances for growth and development. It encourages us to accept difficulties and take chances without fear of failure. It is an attitude that supports creativity, innovation, and advancement.

Failure should be regarded as a learning opportunity rather than a negative event. It allows us to think, evaluate, and learn from our errors, which allows us to develop and thrive in the future. Failure inspires teamwork, resilience, tenacity, and a growth mentality. These are skills that are vital in life and failing gives us the ideal chance to acquire them.

CHAPTER TWO

IDENTIFYING YOUR NICHE

The wellness sector is a fast-increasing market that comprises a broad variety of goods and services meant to enhance optimum health, well-being, and quality of life. This market is fuelled by increased consumer interest and demand for greater health and self-care, as well as the growing popularity of holistic health methods and natural-based goods.

The wellness business may be roughly classified into four primary sectors:

I. Fitness and Nutrition: This sector comprises items and services connected to physical fitness, such as gyms, exercise equipment, supplements, and nutrition programs.

2. Beauty and Personal Care: This sector focuses on items and services that assist people to maintain their physical appearances, such as skincare, hair care, and cosmetics.

3. Alternative Medicine: This includes goods and services based on alternative health approaches, such as acupuncture, chiropractic treatment, and herbal supplements.

4. Mind and Body: This sector emphasizes
the relationship between physical and mental health and provides goods and services that encourage stress reduction, relaxation, and mindfulness, such as yoga

courses, meditation, and massage treatment.

The wellness business is likely to continue increasing, with an estimated market size of over $4 trillion worldwide by 2022. Its increase is driven by numerous reasons, including:

I. Improved Awareness: Consumers are becoming more aware of the need to care for their overall health and well-being, leading to a greater demand for wellness goods and services.

2. Shifting Demographics: As the world population ages, there is a rising demand for goods and services that enhance health and longevity.

3. Technological Advancements: Improvements in technology have made it simpler for wellness enterprises to engage customers and provide individualized wellness plans and programs.

4. Move towards Natural and Organic Products: Many customers are becoming more worried about the influence of synthetic substances on their health, leading to rising demand for natural and organic goods.
Overall, the wellness business is a vibrant and developing market with a broad variety of goods and services targeting customers who are looking to live healthier more balanced lifestyles.

Finding Your Passion
Finding one's passion is a self-discovering journey that leads to the identification of an activity that one likes performing naturally, and that offers a process it needs introspection, critical thinking, and investigation of

numerous interests.

These are some methods to help one identify their passion:

1. Self-reflection: Start by asking yourself what you prefer doing in your leisure time, what comes easily to you, and what motivates you. Reflect on your strengths, values, and what you love doing.

2. Explore your interests: Try out new things and be open to new experiences.
Attend events or programs that interest you, volunteer at different organizations, and immerse yourself in varied surroundings. You may be shocked at what you will find about yourself.

3. Listen to your intuition: Give listen to your inner voice regarding what seems appropriate for you. If you feel enthused and invigorated by a specific activity or topic, it's a positive indicator that you are on the correct route.

4. Take chances: Overcome fear and take risks. Sometimes, the fear of failure holds us back from pursuing our hobbies. Taking prudent risks may help us uncover new elements of ourselves that we never knew existed.

5. Get feedback: Speak to friends, relatives, or individuals who know you well. They may give a new perspective on what they view as your abilities, hobbies, or even things that you may not have considered.

6. Experiment and refine: After you have chosen your passion, experiment* and develop your talents. This

might include enrolling in a course, finding a mentor, or attending seminars to perfect your art.

Discovering your passion is a process that demands a real investigation of oneself. It demands endurance, guts, and patience. Yet discovering your passion is worth it since it may offer a lot of satisfaction, meaning, and pleasure to one's life.

Identifying Your ideal customer could be easy through the use of the following parameters:

1. Demographics: Age, gender, location, income education level, employment, etc.

2. Psychographics: Personality characteristics, values lifestyle, interests, hobbies, attitudes, opinions, etc.

3. Behaviors: Purchasing habits, decision-making process, buying power, spending patterns, communication channels, etc.

4. Pain points: Difficulties, issues, and needs that your target consumer has that you can solve with your product or service.

5. Goals: Goals, ambitions, and aspirations that your ideal customer wishes to attain that correspond with your product or service's solutions.

By knowing these criteria, you can better target and attract your ideal customer, establish marketing techniques that connect with them, and build long-lasting relationships that lead to customer satisfaction and loyalty.

Defining Your Ideal Customer

Identifying your target client is one of the most crucial aspects of developing a successful company. It helps you to discover who your product or service is most suited for and enables you to design a focused marketing plan that connects with your audience. Here are some critical stages to help you identify and understand your target customer:

I. Research: Start by studying your industry, competitors,s and target audience. Search for information on demographics, psychographics, purchasing patterns, needs, and pain spots. You may acquire this information using surveys, interviews, focus groups, or internet research.

2. Identify demographic profile: Look at broad traits that identify your potential consumer. Examine their age, gender, income level, education level, and geographic area. This information can assist you to understand how to adjust your marketing plan to reach your target demographic.

3. Identify psychographics: Go beyond demographics and look at your ideal customer's personality, beliefs, attitudes, interests, and habits. This knowledge can help you understand what inspires your target audience and how to generate message and branding that connects with them.

4. Evaluate their requirements: Identify the difficulties, obstacles, or unfulfilled demands that your potential

consumer is experiencing. Determine how your product or service may address these difficulties and fulfill their demands. This will help you build messaging that speaks directly to them.

5. Build a client persona: After you have collected all the essential information, construct a customer persona that portrays your ideal customer. This persona should have a namer's age, work position, hobbies, pain spots, and shopping behaviors. This will provide you with a greater insight into your target demographic and help you build marketing efforts that are targeted and powerful.

6. Constantly obtain feedback: Lastly, continue to gather feedback from your target group to enhance your customer persona and marketing plan. Utilize consumer feedback to alter your message product functionality, and other parts of your company to better line with your target demographic.

Identifying your ideal consumer is a continual process that includes regular study, listening, and testing. By knowing and responding to the demands of your ideal consumer, you can develop a strong brand and generate a loyal customer base.

CHAPTER THREE

CREATING A BUSINESS PLAN

C hoosing the corporate structure for a wellness firm needs careful consideration of various variables, including business objectives, ownership, responsibility, taxes, and regulatory compliance. Following are some of the most frequent company forms in the wellness industry:

Sole Proprietorship: A sole proprietorship is the simplest business form, and it comprises one individual owning and running the firm. This form is appropriate for small wellness enterprises, such as yoga studios or massage treatment operations. The owner has entire control over the company, but they are personally accountable for any debts or legal troubles.

Partnership: A partnership comprises two or more persons owning and running the firm. Partnerships may be general, where all partners participate equally in the profits and losses or limited when one partner has limited responsibility. Partnerships are ideal for businesses that require specialized expertise, such as nutrition counseling or fitness coaching.

Limited Liability Company (LLC): An LLC is a hybrid structure that combines the benefits of a partnership and a corporation. LLCs provide liability protection for the owners, meaning they are not personally liable for any debts or legal issues. LLCs are ideal for wellness businesses that want to protect their assets while maintaining flexibility in management and taxation.

Corporation: A corporation is a separate legal entity from its owners, and it provides the most significant liability protection for the owners. However, corporations are subject to more complex taxation and regulation, and they require significant resources to establish and maintain. Corporations are ideal for large wellness companies that plan to raise capital through investors and expand their business internationally.

Nonprofit: A nonprofit is a business structure that is tax-exempt and operates for a charitable or social purpose. Nonprofits are perfect for wellness enterprises that concentrate on community services, such as giving free health screenings or education programs.

Choosing the right business structure for a wellness company requires careful consideration of the business goals, ownership, liability, taxation, and regulatory compliance. Business owners should consult with legal and financial experts to determine the best structure for their business.

Developing Short-Term and Long-Term Goals
Developing short-term and long-term goals is essential for any wellness business to succeed. Short-term goals help the business achieve quick wins and build momentum, while long-term goals provide direction and focus for the business's growth and sustainability. Here are some examples of short-term and long-term goals for a wellness business:

Short-term goals:
Increase social media presence: Create and post regular content on social media platforms to attract and engage with customers.

Host a community event: Organize a health and wellness event, such as a charity walk, to build brand awareness and connect with the local community.

Offer a promotional deal: Offer discounts or special deals to attract new customers and retain existing ones.

Expand service offerings: Add new services, such as nutritional counseling or meditation classes, to attract a broader range of customers.

Improve customer service: Train staff to provide excellent customer service to improve customer satisfaction and retention.
Long-term goals:

Expand to multiple locations: Establish new
wellness facilities or studios in various places to enhance income and market share.

Establish a loyalty program: Build a loyalty program to reward regular customers and promote repeat business.

Establish a referral program: Motivate current customers to suggest friends and family to the company by giving rewards.

Create a brand identity: Create a strong brand identity via consistent message, visual branding, and customer experience.

Adopt a sustainability strategy: Create a sustainability plan to decrease the business's environmental effects and promote social responsibility.

Short-term and long-term objectives are crucial for a wellness business's success. Company owners should develop reasonable objectives that correspond with their vision and purpose and frequently evaluate and alter them to guarantee continuing growth and success

Financial Planning

Financial planning is a critical aspect of creating and sustaining a successful wellness company. It entails designing a financial roadmap to meet the business's short-term and long-term objectives, manage cash flow, and allocate resources efficiently. Here are some critical aspects to consider when building a financial strategy for your wellness business:

Establish financial goals: Set clear financial objectives that connect with the business's vision and purpose, such as revenue targets, profit margins, and return on investment. Ensure that these objectives are precise, measurable, attainable, relevant, and time-bound (SMART) (SMART).

Perform a financial analysis: Evaluate the business's financial accounts, including income statements, balance sheets, and cash flow statements, to identify strengths, weaknesses, opportunities, and threats. Utilize this study to make educated financial choices and build methods to reduce financial risks.

Establish a budget: Create a thorough budget that details

the business's planned income, costs, and cash flow. Incorporate all fixed and variable expenditures, such as rent, wages, marketing, and inventory. Monitor and revise the budget often to ensure the firm continues on track.

Control cash flow: Ensure that the firm has adequate cash on hand to meet its costs and investments. Employ effective cash flow management practices, such as prompt invoicing, inventory management, and credit management.

Invest in technology: Employ technological solutions, such as financial management software, online booking systems, and customer relationship management (CRM) tools, to simplify operations, cut expenses, and enhance customer service.

Get financial advice: Engage with financial specialists, such as accountants, financial advisers, and business consultants, to gain professional assistance and help. They may give useful insights into financial planning, taxes, and compliance issues.

Financial preparation is crucial for creating and maintaining a successful wellness company. It entails defining clear financial objectives, doing financial analysis, making a budget, controlling cash flow, investing in technology, and getting expert guidance. Company owners should emphasize financial planning as a vital business activity and frequently evaluate and adapt their financial plans to guarantee sustained development and success.

CHAPTER FOUR

BUILDING BRAND AWARENESS

Developing a strong brand identity is vital for a wellness company to stand out in a competitive field and attract and keep clients. A brand identity encompasses the visual and non-visual elements that represent the business, such as its name, logo, messaging, values, and customer experience. Here are some key steps to consider when establishing a strong brand identity for your wellness business:

Define your brand: Start by defining your brand's purpose, values, and personality. Evaluate your target audience, competitors, and industry trends. Create a distinctive brand positioning that separates your firm from competitors in the market.

Develop a striking visual identity: Create a visual identity that matches your brand's mission, beliefs, and personality. This involves establishing a distinctive logo, choosing a color scheme, and designing a website, signage, and marketing materials that represent your brand's appearance and feel.

Create a consistent messaging plan: Establish a messaging strategy that expresses your brand's mission, values, and personality consistently across all communication platforms. This involves designing intriguing taglines, headlines, and calls to action that connects with your target audience.

Concentrate on the customer experience: Emphasis on creating a unique and great customer experience that matches your brand's mission, values, and personality. This involves offering high-quality services, fostering a welcoming and inclusive atmosphere, and connecting with consumers in a meaningful manner.

Employ social media and content marketing: Utilize social media and content marketing to boost brand recognition and connect with consumers. Create a content plan that resonates with your brand's mission, beliefs, and personality, and disseminate it through social media platforms, blogs, and email newsletters.

Utilize partnerships and sponsorships: Leverage partnerships and sponsorships with other companies and organizations that connect with your brand's mission, values, and personality. This may help you reach new audiences and create brand trust.

Building a strong brand identity is vital for a wellness company to prosper. It entails establishing your brand, building a compelling visual identity, having a consistent message strategy, concentrating on the customer experience, employing social media and content marketing, and leveraging partnerships and sponsorships. Company owners should prioritize creating a strong brand identity as a fundamental business function and periodically assess and adapt their brand strategy to guarantee sustained development and success.

Identifying and Reaching Your Target Audience

Defining and targeting your target audience is a vital component of marketing for any company, including wellness enterprises. A target audience is a set of individuals who are more likely to be interested in your goods or services and who are more likely to become loyal clients. These are some crucial considerations to consider when selecting and contacting your target audience:

Do market research: Do market research to understand your target audience's demographics, psychographics, habits, and preferences. This involves studying industry trends, evaluating consumer data, and conducting surveys and focus groups.

Create buyer personas: Build buyer personas that describe your target audience's qualities, wants, and ambitions. This helps you understand their pain points, motives, and habits and design tailored marketing tactics that connect with them.

Segment your audience: Segment your audience depending on their demographics, habits, and interests. This enables you to adjust your marketing messages and methods to each group's requirements and preferences.

Utilize social media: Use social media to reach your target demographic. Create a social media plan that involves developing targeted advertisements, communicating with followers, and posting relevant information.

Create content marketing: Build content marketing techniques that connect with your target audience. This includes creating blog posts, videos, and other types of content that address their pain points and offer solutions to their problems.

Participate in community events: Participate in community events that align with your brand's values and attract your target audience. This includes sponsoring events, speaking at conferences, and hosting workshops.

Leverage email marketing: Leverage email marketing to reach your target audience. Develop targeted email campaigns that provide value to your subscribers and encourage them to engage with your business.

Use paid advertising: Use paid advertising, such as Google AdWords, Facebook Ads, and Instagram Ads, to reach your target audience. Develop targeted campaigns that reach people who are most likely to be interested in your products or services.

Identifying and reaching your target audience is essential for a wellness business to succeed. It involves conducting market research, developing buyer personas, segmenting your audience, using social media, developing content marketing, participating in community events, leveraging email marketing, and using paid advertising. Business owners should prioritize understanding and engage with their target audience as a core business function and regularly review and adjust their marketing strategies to ensure continued growth and success.

Developing a Marketing Strategy

Creating a marketing plan is vital for every company, especially wellness enterprises. A marketing strategy explains the way a firm uses to advertise its goods or services, attracts retaining consumers, and eventually grgrowsvenue. These are some crucial steps to consider while building a marketing strategy:

Do market research: Perform market research to understand your target audience's requirements, preferences, and habits. This involves studying industry trends, customer data, and competition information.

Define your distinct value proposition: Establish your unique value proposition, which is the fundamental feature that sets your firm different from the competitors. This should be straightforward and persuasive and address your target audience's pain concerns.

Establish marketing goals: Create marketing goals that match your business's overall aims. This involves creating clear, measurable, attainable, relevant, and time-bound (SMART) objectives.

Create a marketing mix: Build a marketing mix that encompasses the four Ps of marketing: product, pricing, location, and promotion. This comprises establishing your product or service offering, price plan, distribution methods, and promotional strategies.

Develop a messaging plan: Build a messaging strategy that expresses your unique value offer and resonates with your target audience. This involves establishing a slogan, goal statement, and elevator pitch.

Create a content plan: Build a content strategy that supports your message approach and gives value to your target audience. This involves writing blog articles, videos, social media postings, and other sorts of content that target your audience's pain spots and give answers to their issues.

Employ marketing strategies: Adopt marketing methods that correspond with your marketing mix, message strategy, and content strategy. This involves leveraging social media, email marketing, paid advertising, search engine optimization (SEO), and public relations (PR) (PR).

Assess and adapt: Evaluate the efficacy of your marketing approach and alter your techniques as appropriate. This involves measuring key performance indicators (KPIs), such as website traffic, lead generation, conversion rates, and client retention.

Building a marketing plan is vital for a wellness company to prosper. It comprises performing market research, establishing your unique value proposition, setting marketing objectives, constructing a marketing mix, creating a message strategy, developing a content strategy, applying marketing methods, and monitoring and changing your approach. Company owners should prioritize building a marketing strategy as a vital business function and frequently assess and adapt their approach to guarantee sustained development and success.

CHAPTER FIVE

BUILDING YOUR NETWORK

Developing ties with other entrepreneurs is vital for company success, particularly in the wellness sector where cooperation and partnerships may lead to improved brand visibility and income. Here are some crucial measures to consider while creating partnerships with other entrepreneurs:

Attend networking events: Attend networking events in your field to meet and interact with other entrepreneurs. This covers industry conferences, trade exhibits, and local business events.

Join industry associations: Join industry organizations and clubs to network with other entrepreneurs and receive access to tools and information that may help you build your firm.

Utilize social media: Use social media to connect with other entrepreneurs in your sector. This involves following industry experts on Twitter, joining LinkedIn groups, and engaging in online debates.

Collaborate on initiatives: Work with other entrepreneurs on projects that correspond with your company objectives. This includes co-hosting events, cooperating on marketing initiatives, and delivering combined services or goods.

Share resources: Share resources with other businesses

to create trust and promote yourself as a useful partner. This involves sharing industry knowledge, making recommendations, and providing mentoring.

Join mastermind groups: Attend mastermind groups to network with other entrepreneurs and acquire insights into business best practices and tactics.

Attend workshops and seminars: Attend workshops and seminars to learn from other entrepreneurs and get new skills that may help you build your company.

Help other entrepreneurs: Assist other entrepreneurs by sharing their material, providing comments, and promoting their goods or services. This might help you create connections and generate a great reputation in the business.

Creating ties with other entrepreneurs is vital for acompanyasuccess susuccessfulmarket. By developing ties with other entrepreneurs, you may get access to resources and information that can help you expand your firm, while also building a network of trustworthy partners and collaborators.

Collaborating With Other Businesses
Collaborating with other businesses can be a powerful way to grow your wellness business. When businesses collaborate, they can pool resources, share knowledge and expertise, and reach new audiences. Here are some key steps to consider when collaborating with other businesses:

Identify potential partners: Identify potential partners

that share similar values, target audiences, and complementary services or products. This might include firms in the same industry or comparable sectors.

Identify goals and objectives: Establish explicit goals and objectives for the cooperation, including what each side intends to accomplish and how success will be judged.

Determine roles and responsibilities: Define the roles and duties of each participant in the partnership, including who will be accountable for certain areas of the project and how decisions will be made.

Create a plan: Create a strategy for the partnership, timetable, budget, and resources required. This should include clear communication routes and protocols for resolving any difficulties that may occur.

Communicate effectively: Speak often and freely with your partners to ensure that everyone is on the same page and any concerns are resolved swiftly. This involves setting up frequent meetings, discussing progress updates, and resolving any problems that may emerge.

Foster trust: Build trust amongst partners by being truthful, dependable, and collaborative. This requires being receptive to comments, sharing information and skills, and valuing each other's contributions.

Assess and adjust: Assess the success of the partnership and adapt your strategy as appropriate. This entails reviewing the outcomes against the goals and objectives, finding areas for improvement, and implementing adjustments to guarantee continuous success.

Examples of cooperation in the wellness business include:

- Co-hosting events, such as seminars, courses, or webinars
- Providing collaborative services or goods, such as health retreats or bundled services
- Sharing marketing resources, such as email lists or social media followers
- Offering suggestions for comparable services or products
- Collaboration on research or development projects

Cooperating with other firms might be an efficient strategy to build your wellness company. By working with other businesses, you can leverage their resources and expertise to reach new audiences, increase revenue, and achieve your business goals.

Utilize the Social Media

Social media may be a tremendous tool for building your wellness company, as it enables you to interact with new consumers, create connections, and market your goods and services. These are some crucial considerations to consider while using social media:

Select the correct platforms: Select the social media sites that are most relevant to your company and target demographic. This might include networks such as Instagram, Facebook, Twitter, LinkedIn, or YouTube.

Develop a content strategy: Create a content strategy

that corresponds with your company objectives and target audience. This should include the sorts of material you will develop (such as blog entries, videos, or infographics), how frequently you will publish, and what themes you will cover.

Create a community: Create a community by participating with your followers, replying to comments and messages, and sharing material from other users. This may help you gain trust, establish yourself as an authority, and expand your following.

Employ images: Utilize visuals such as photographs, movies, and graphics to make your material more engaging and memorable. This might help you stand out from the competition and attract the attention of prospective clients.

Employ hashtags: Utilize relevant hashtags to boost the exposure of your content and reach a broader audience. This might help you connect with individuals who are interested in your topic and enhance interaction with your material.

Promote your goods and services: Promote your products and services by presenting their features, advantages, and unique selling factors. This can help you generate leads and increase sales.

Analyze your results: Analyze your social media metrics to measure the success of your efforts and identify areas for improvement. This could include tracking engagement, follower growth, website traffic, and sales.

Some additional tips for utilizing social media include:

-     Create a social media calendar to plan and schedule your posts in advance
-    Experiment with different types of content to see what resonates with your audience
-     Use social media advertising to reach a wider audience and generate leads
-    Collaborate with other businesses and influencers to increase your reach and credibility

Utilizing social media can be a powerful way to grow your wellness business. By effectively utilizing social media, you can connect with potential customers, build relationships, and promote your business cost-effectively and measurably

CHAPTER SIX

MANAGING TIME AND RESOURCES

Effective time management is crucial for running a successful wellness business. It enables you to remain organized, enhance productivity, and accomplish your objectives. These are some major time management tactics that may be employed:

Prioritize tasks: Prioritize your chores by finding the most critical and urgent ones. This might help you concentrate on the things that have the biggest influence on your company and prevent spending time on less critical chores.

Make a schedule: Establish a calendar that contains dedicated time blocks for certain duties, such as answering emails, writing content, and working on client projects. This may help you keep on task and avoid distractions.

Utilize tools and technology: Utilize tools and technologies to improve your workflow and automate repetitive processes. These might include project management tools, scheduling software, and social media management services.

Delegate tasks: Assign jobs to team members or freelancers to free up your time and concentrate on the things that need your skills. This may also help you strengthen your team members' talents and boost their involvement.

Take pauses: Take breaks often to minimize burnout and increase your overall productivity. This might involve taking a brief stroll, practicing mindfulness, or indulging in a pastime that helps you recharge.

Avoid multitasking: Avoid multitasking, since it might lower your productivity and raise your stress levels. Instead, concentrate on one activity at a time and accomplish it before moving on to the next one.

Assess your progress: Assess your progress often to find areas for improvement and alter your strategy as appropriate. This might entail monitoring your time, reviewing your outcomes, and collecting feedback from customers or team members.

Some more ideas for good time management include:
- Establish reasonable timelines and objectives
- Minimize procrastination by dividing major activities into smaller ones
- Employ the Pomodoro method to increase attention and productivity
- Learn to say no to jobs or initiatives that do not correspond with your company's aims or values

Efficient time management is vital for operating a successful health company. By applying these tactics, you may boost your productivity, minimize stress, and accomplish your business objectives.

Managing Finances and Resources

Handling funds and resources is a vital component of establishing a successful health company. It entails accurate budgeting, managing spending, and making educated choices regarding investments and resource distribution. Here are some critical ideas for managing cash and resources as a health entrepreneur:

Establish a budget: Establish a budget that accounts for all of your company expenditures, such as rent, utilities, marketing, supplies, and wages. This might help you focus your expenditures and prevent overpaying in some areas.

Track expenses: Monitor your spending frequently to remain on top of your cash flow and uncover areas where you may minimize costs. This might involve utilizing accounting software, such as Quickbooks, to manage to spend and provide financial reports.

Monitor income streams: Analyze your revenue streams to find areas of growth and make educated choices regarding investments. This might entail assessing sales data, monitoring consumer comments, and watching industry trends.

Create a cash reserve: Establish a cash reserve to prepare for unforeseen costs or sluggish times. This might involve saving away a portion of your sales each month or acquiring a line of credit or company loan.

Invest strategically: Invest strategically in areas that offer the greatest potential for development and return on investment. This might involve investing in new goods or services, boosting your marketing activities, or recruiting extra workers.

Negotiate contracts and agreements: Negotiate contracts and agreements with suppliers and partners to guarantee you are receiving the most value for your money. This could include negotiating lower prices or longer payment terms.

Handle resources efficiently: Manage your resources, such as time and staff, efficiently to maximize productivity and reduce waste.
This could include implementing systems and processes that streamline workflows, outsourcing tasks to freelancers, or cross-training staff to increase their versatility.

Some more strategies for managing funds and resources include:

- Stay informed about changes in tax laws and regulations
- Develop a contingency plan in case of unexpected events, such as a pandemic or natural disaster
- Seek the advice of a financial professional, such as an accountant or financial advisor, to ensure you are making informed decisions

Managing finances and resources is a critical aspect of running a successful wellness business. It involves creating a budget and tracking it.

Dealing with Burnout

Burnout is a condition of emotional, mental, and physical weariness produced by continuous exposure to stress. It is a frequent condition, particularly in today's fast-paced and demanding culture, and it may affect anybody regardless of career or age. Coping with burnout takes a multi-faceted strategy that incorporates self-care, stress management, and getting professional assistance when required.

Recognizing the indications of burnout:
The first step in coping with burnout is to identify the indicators. Burnout symptoms may vary from person to person, but some frequent indicators include:

- Persistent weariness and exhaustion
- Feeling overwhelmed and powerless
- Lack of enthusiasm and interest in work or other activities
- Insomnia or trouble sleeping
- Increased irritation and frustration
- Decreased performance and productivity
- Physical problems such as headaches, backaches, and gastrointestinal troubles.

Practice self-care:\sSelf-care is vital in coping with burnout. It means taking care of oneself physically, emotionally, and psychologically.

Some self-care techniques include:
- Obtaining enough sleep and rest
- Eating a healthy and balanced diet
- Participating in physical activity, such as exercise or yoga
- Using relaxation methods, such as meditation or deep breathing

- Spending time with loved ones and participating in social activities
- Taking getaways and holidays to refresh and renew.

Handle stress:
Handling stress is another key component of coping with burnout. Stress is typically the underlying cause of burnout, and it's crucial to recognize and manage stress triggers.

Some stress management approaches include:
- Establishing limits and saying no to unreasonable requests
- Prioritizing activities and allocating responsibilities
- Building excellent time management abilities
- Cultivating mindfulness and remaining present at the moment
- Seeking support from friends, family, or colleagues.

Get expert assistance:\sInn certain circum In coping with burnout may need professional treatment. A mental health expert, such as a therapist or counselor, may give direction and assistance in managing stress and resolving underlying emotional difficulties. Several kinds of treatment that may be useful for burnout include cognitive-behavioral therapy, mindfulness-based stress reduction, and psychodynamic therapy.

In short, coping with burnout takes a multi-faceted strategy that entails identifying the indications, practicing self-care, reducing stress, and getting professional assistance when required. It's crucial to prioritize your well-being and take action to avoid burnout before it becomes a chronic and severe problem.

CHAPTER SEVEN

BUILDING A STRONG TEAM

I dentifying and recruiting the proper staff is a vital element of developing a successful company. It entails defining the precise skills and traits required for each job, seeking and attracting individuals, and assessing them to guarantee a good match with the company's culture and values. These are some steps to take in discovering and recruiting the ideal employees:

Specify the job requirements:
The first step in locating the ideal workers is to identify the job criteria. This comprises defining the relevant abilities, expertise, and credentials needed for the post. It's crucial to be explicit and realistic about what the work requires and what sort of individual would be the greatest match for the post.

Source candidates:
After you have specified the job criteria, you need to discover suitable applicants. There are several techniques to source applicants, including:

- Placing job adverts on employment boards or social media
- Utilizing recruitment agencies or headhunters
- About employee referrals
- Networking via industry events or LinkedIn.
- Evaluate resumes and applications:

After finding applicants, the next step is to analyze their resumes and applications. Seek applicants that have the essential abilities and experience, as well as a history of success in past employment. Take attention to their schooling, employment background, and any applicable qualifications or achievements.

Conduct interviews:
After you have discovered possible applicants, it's time to conduct interviews. The interview process is a chance to get to know the applicants better and assess their fit with the firm. Create a list of questions that will help you evaluate their abilities, experience, and cultural fit.

Check references:
Before making a final hiring decision, it's important to check references. Call their prior employers or coworkers to validate their job history and get a feel of their character and work style.

Make an offer:After the interview process and reference checks, if you have identified the perfect applicant, it's time to make an offer. Be specific about the conditions of employment, such as pay, benefits, and start date.

Onboard and train:Once the applicant has accepted the offer, it's vital to onboard and train them. This involves introducing them to the corporate culture, rules, and processes, as well as providing them with the required training and tools to succeed in their new capacity.

In summary, selecting and employing the ideal workers needs rigorous preparation, sourcing, and assessment.

By establishing job needs, sourcing individuals, examining resumes and applications, conducting interviews, verifying references, making an offer, and onboarding and training new workers, you can develop a solid team that will help your company prosper.

Developing a Positive Workplace Culture

Establishing a healthy workplace culture is vital for any company, particularly for wellness entrepreneurs who are enthusiastic about promoting health and well-being. Healthy workplace culture may contribute to higher employee engagement, productivity, and job satisfaction, which ultimately benefits both the workers and the organization. Here are some strategies for developing a great working culture as a wellness entrepreneur:

Describe your beliefs and mission:

The first step in creating a positive workplace culture is to define your values and mission. These should be aligned with your wellness business's vision and goals. Communicate your values and mission to your employees, and ensure that everyone is on board with the company's purpose.

Foster a supportive and inclusive environment:A positive workplace culture should be supportive and inclusive. Establish an atmosphere where workers feel appreciated, respected, and comfortable expressing themselves. Promote teamwork, cooperation, and open communication. Guarantee that everyone has an equal opportunity for growth and development.

Emphasize employee well-being:\sAs a wellness

entrepreneur, emphasizing employee well-being should be at the center of your company principles. Cultivate a good work-life balance by giving flexible work arrangements, paid time off, and employee wellness initiatives. Encourage staff to take breaks, walk outdoors, and exercise self-care.

Acknowledge and reward employee successes:Recognizing and recognizing employee achievements is vital for developing a strong workplace culture. Appreciate victories, both large and little, and recognize workers' contributions to the organization. Give rewards and bonuses for exemplary achievement, and promote peer-to-peer recognition.

Offer chances for learning and development:
Investing in your workers' learning and development is a strong strategy to establish a pleasant workplace culture. Offer training and development programs to help employees grow professionally and personally. Encourage them to attend conferences, workshops, and other relevant events to broaden their knowledge and skills.

Lead by example:
As a wellness entrepreneur, you are the leader of your business, and your actions set the tone for the workplace culture. Lead by example by practicing what you preach. Show your employees that you prioritize well-being, work-life balance, and positive relationships. Be transparent, honest, and respectful in your interactions with employees.

In summary, creating a positive workplace culture as a wellness entrepreneur requires defining your values and mission, fostering a supportive and inclusive environment, prioritizing employee well-being, recognizing and rewarding employee achievements, providing opportunities for learning and development, and leading by example. By implementing these practices, you can build a positive and thriving workplace culture that benefits everyone in the business.

Training and Empowering Team Members

As a wellness coach, your success is mainly based on your ability to teach and empower your team members. By doing so, you may establish a strong staff that is skilled, confident, and capable of helping your customers in accomplishing their health and wellness objectives. Here are some strategies for training and empowering your team members as a hhealthcoacoachhhhealthhhblish explicit roles and responsibilities:

To empower your team members, it's necessary to create defined roles and duties. This will assist people to understand their specific contributions to the team and how they fit into the overarching objective of the organization. Be clear about what is expected of each team member and give frequent feedback to assist them to improve their performance.

Provide training and development chances:\sTo assist your team members to grow and improve, give training and development opportunities. Training may include on-the-job training, coaching, and mentoring programs. Give access to materials such as books, articles, and online courses that may help people enhance their knowledge and abilities.

Promote cooperation and teamwork: Empowering your team members demands building a collaborative and supportive team culture. Encourage your team members to contribute their ideas, thoughts, and experiences. Provide chances for cooperation and collaboration, such as team meetings, brainstorming sessions, and group projects.

Provide constructive feedback: To help your team members improve their performance, provide constructive feedback. Be detailed, impartial, and timely in your criticism. Concentrate on behaviors and deeds rather than personal attributes. Give comments in a manner that is courteous and helpful.

Distribute duties: To empower your team members, assign tasks and enable them to take responsibility for their job. This will help them grow their talents and confidence while also freeing up their time to concentrate on other elements of the firm. Be upfront about expectations and give the necessary assistance and resources to help them achieve.

Acknowledge and reward successes: Recognizing and praising your team members' achievements is vital for developing a culture of empowerment. Appreciate victories, both large and little, and recognize the efforts of each team member. Give rewards and bonuses for exemplary achievement, and promote peer-to-peer recognition.

By applying these principles, you may establish a strong and competent team that helps your customers in attaining their health and wellness objectives.

CHAPTER EIGHT

SCALING YOUR BUSINESS

As a wellness entrepreneur, having a growth plan is vital for growing your company and reaching additional consumers. A growth plan explains the measures you will take to develop your firm, boost your income, and accomplish your objectives. Here are some recommendations for building a development plan as a wellness entrepreneur:

Define your goals:
The first step in designing a development plan is to identify your objectives. Determine what you want to accomplish, such as raising your income, extending your customer base, or releasing new goods or services. Your objectives should be defined, quantifiable, and reachable within a set period.

Do market research: To build a growth plan, you need to understand your target market and competitors. Perform market research to uncover trends, client preferences, and gaps in the industry. Study your competitors to find their strengths and flaws, and how you might separate yourself from them.

Determine your unique selling proposal: To stand out in a competitive market, you need to have a unique selling proposition (USP) (USP). Determine what sets your firm distinct from others and how you may convey this to your target market. Your USP might be your knowledge, a certain technique or approach, or the quality of your goods or services.

Create a marketing strategy: Once you have established your objectives, completed market research, and determined your USP, build a marketing plan to reach your target market. Your marketing strategy should contain tactics for promoting your company via numerous channels, such as social media, email marketing, content marketing, and advertising.

Develop a sales plan: To improve your income and build your firm, you need a sales strategy. This might involve designing a sales funnel, providing upsells and cross-sells, or generating packages and promotions to motivate customers to buy more from you.

Recruit and train team members: As your firm expands, you may need to employ team members to help you. Employ team members who share your values and objectives and who have the skills and expertise essential to help you reach your goals. Teach your team members to ensure they understand your company, your goods or services, and your procedures.

Monitor and analyze your progress:
To guarantee your development plan is functioning, review and analyze your progress periodically. Put up key performance indicators (KPIs) to assess your progress toward your objectives, such as revenue growth, client acquisition, and customer retention. Utilize this data to change your plan By adopting these steps, you can develop a profitable and sustainable

wellness company.

Expanding Your Product and Service Offerings

Increasing your product and service offerings is a crucial step towards developing your wellness company and improving your income. By broadening your products, you may appeal to a larger spectrum of consumers and deliver more value to your current clientele. Here are some strategies for growing your product and service offerings:

Determine your target market:
Before you extend your products, it's crucial to establish your target market. Who are your ideal customers, and what are their wants and preferences? Knowing your target market can assist you to select which items and services to provide.

Assess your competition:
To separate yourself from your competitors, it's vital to examine their products. What goods and services do they provide, and how can you offer something unique or better? This can help you find gaps in the market and chances for development.

Do market research:
Doing market research may help you understand client preferences, discover trends, and get input on prospective new offers. This might involve surveys, focus groups, or interviews with your current consumers.

Create a product or service plan: Once you have discovered possible new offerings, build a strategy for creating and releasing them. This should contain schedules, budgets, and resources necessary. Prioritize products based on their potential influence on revenue and customer happiness.

Test and refine: Before introducing a new product or service, it's vital to test and refine it. This might entail delivering a beta version to a restricted set of clients or running a pilot campaign. Collect feedback and utilize it to develop your service before releasing it to a broader audience.

Utilize partnerships and collaborations: Partnering with other firms or people in the wellness sector may help you grow your products and reach new clients. This might entail working on a new product or service, co-marketing efforts, or cross-promotion.

Constantly assess and iterate:
Growing your offerings is a constant process that demands regular examination and iteration. Analyze customer feedback, sales statistics, and market trends to discover areas for improvement and possible new offers.

Applying these methods will help you expand your offers and build your wellness company.

Establishing New Partnerships
Forming partnerships is a fantastic method for wellness coaches to increase their reach, give additional value to customers, and build their companies. Here are some ways for creating new collaborations as a health coach:

Identify possible partners:

Start by finding possible partners in the wellness business. Search for firms or people whose services match your own and who share your beliefs and purpose. They might be yoga studios, fitness facilities, health food shops, wellness retreats, or other wellness experts.

Research possible partners:
After you have discovered possible partners, explore them to learn more about their companies and offers. Look for prospects for cooperation or cooperative marketing activities. Call out to them to introduce yourself and explain why you believe a collaboration might be helpful.

Create a cooperation proposal:
When engaging prospective partners, it's crucial to have a clear proposition articulating the advantages of a relationship. Describe how cooperation might assist both sides to attain their objectives, and how it could benefit their consumers. Be explicit about what you can provide, and what you are seeking in exchange.

Collaborate on a pilot program:
Before committing to a long-term collaboration, it's a good idea to work on a trial initiative to test the waters. This might entail presenting a collaborative workshop, class, or event to your united consumer base. Collect comments and statistics to assess the performance of the pilot program and decide if long-term cooperation is possible.

Define partnership terms:

After you have built a successful pilot program, it's necessary to clarify the terms of the agreement. This might include income sharing, collaborative marketing campaigns, and how each partner will contribute to the alliance.

Communicate and collaborate:
Effective communication and teamwork are vital to a successful relationship. Frequently contact base with your partner to share success, issues, and possibilities for development. Collaborate on cooperative marketing activities, such as social media campaigns, email marketing, or events.
Assess and adjust:
Like every business venture, partnerships need frequent examination and change. Evaluate the performance of the collaboration over time, and alter the terms and strategy as appropriate. Constantly obtain input from consumers and partners to verify the collaboration is satisfying their requirements.

In summary, establishing new partnerships as a wellness coach requires identifying potential partners, researching them, developing a partnership proposal, collaborating on a pilot program, defining partnership terms, communicating and collaborating effectively, and evaluating and adjusting over time. By following these steps, you can develop effective relationships that benefit both you and your partners, and help you expand your wellness company.

Final Word

Starting a wellness business can be a daunting task, but with the right mindset, attitude, and actions, you can achieve great success. Here are some words of encouragement to help you take action and succeed in your wellness entrepreneurship

Believing in yourself: The first step to success in health entrepreneurship is believing in yourself. Trust your intuition and have trust in your ability. Remember that every great entrepreneur began from someplace, and with hard work, drive, and enthusiasm, you too can reach your objectives.

Concentrate on your purpose and values: To thrive in wellness entrepreneurship, it's crucial to have a clear mission and values. Explain what you stand for, what you aim to accomplish, and how you want to affect the world. Concentrate on generating goods and services that match your vision and beliefs, and that serve your consumers.

Accept failure as a learning opportunity: Not every business effort will be successful, and that's alright. Accept failure as a learning opportunity, and utilize it to make better choices in the future. Don't be afraid to take chances, and don't allow fear of failure to keep you back.

Surround yourself with supporting individuals: Surround yourself with supportive people who believe in you and your goals. Seek mentors, join networking organizations, and surround yourself with like-minded persons who can give direction and support along the road.

Be inquisitive and adaptive: In the ever-changing world of wellness entrepreneurship, it's crucial to remain curious and adaptable. Stay up with the current trends and advancements in the sector, and be open to new ideas and methods. Don't be scared to pivot or alter your company strategy as required.

Taking action: Success in the wellness business demands taking action. Don't wait for the ideal time or the perfect strategy. Start small, take persistent action, and learn as you go. Concentrate on making progress every day, and enjoy your triumphs along the way.

Practice self-care: As a health entrepreneur, it's crucial to practice what you preach. Take care of yourself, both physically and psychologically, and prioritize self-care. Remember that your well-being and happiness are just as vital as your company's success.

In summary, success in wellness entrepreneurship entails believing in yourself, concentrating on your goal and beliefs, accepting failure as a learning opportunity, surrounding yourself with supportive people, keeping inquisitive and adaptive, taking action, and practicing self-care. With these words of encouragement in mind, go out and follow your aspirations, and know that success is within your grasp.

www.ingramcontent.com/pod-product-compliance
Lightning Source LLC
Chambersburg PA
CBHW071143220526
45467CB00015B/1789